HAIKU POND

Since leaving,
Not yet—
"*My life has been the poem*
I would have writ . . ."*

*Thoreau, poem, 1841

HAIKU POND

A trace of the trail . . .

and Thoreau

by Vincent Tripi

Illustrations by Linda C. Kneeland

Author's Note

All profits from the sale of this book will be rendered to The Thoreau Society, Inc. 156 Belknap Street, Concord, Massachusetts 01742. Walter Harding, Secretary.

Signed copies may be ordered at additional cost (postage and handling) from the author to Vide Press, 478 A Second Avenue, San Francisco, California 94118.

Vide Press
478 A Second Avenue
San Francisco, California 94118

Cover design by Linda C. Kneeland
Cover illustration by Linda C. Kneeland
Book design by Sarah Levin
Typeset by Wilsted & Taylor
Printed by Edwards Brothers

Library of Congress Catalogue Card
Number: 87-051003
ISBN: 0-9619134-0-1

Printed in the United States of America
10 9 8 7 6 5 4 3 2 1

To Matthew and Peter
who watched the bullfrog
swim away.

$\dfrac{\text{Half}}{\text{Bullfrog}}$ . . . . . . Drops
In my eye!

CONTENTS

ILLUSTRATIONS

P R E F A C E

Full Trail

Without beginning, hat down and weave between the vine. Silence takes over, the mountain takes over, . . . enough of a dragonfly's wing.

Towhees from a bush, feet-shifting, red into sky. Harebells clustered in a great hush facing south. A frog is . . . because the pond is round.

Cloud-above, or below, the dew is dripping—from a loon's beak waiting for the sun. Its name was Medawisla,* for this was a sign of the wind.

Granite-again.

Moonstone, breathstone . . . full-trail on me now.

Here at the pond I learned how to write, when I finally had learned how to pray!

Journal
October 5, 1984

PONDtipofapen!

"But that New Hampshire bluff,—that promontory of a State,—lowering day and night on this our State of Massachusetts, will longest haunt our dreams."

THOREAU
A Walk to Wachusett

*from Thoreau—an Indian word for the loon.

INTRODUCTION

The pond is Her beginning.
Eternal ripples, each . . . on their Way
Round the world!

Nature is forever, just because it's always disappearing. This-way! That-way!—the wind not proud of fragrance, the rocks not proud of mountains, giving light.

We are part of the pond, part of Her secrets . . . the breathless-winding secrets: joyous belonging, thunder from a shell, and water where we stand to be revealed.

I offer this work in my 44th year, knowing that Thoreau was the same age when he died, and knowing too that "The Thoreau Society" was founded in the month that I was born.

However old, "maturity" (as for Thoreau) could never mean the loss of wonder. His sensitivity to Nature was such that he almost always was surprised by the ordinary events of our life. It was in his own immediacy of discovery that he began to discover himself.

In this book there is a very close relationship between journal entries, artwork, haiku, and quotations from Thoreau, which helps to generate a specific mood or sensation that could not otherwise be evoked.

Each page becomes "a picture"—the pond "infinity", the symbols "life", and the poems and art "the spark" that make them one.

Rather than recording abstractions, it is my intention to provide the reader with a "full impression" of each moment as it happens . . . to flame the strength that comes from every contact with the earth.

Wherever the words "sit" or "sitting" appear in my journal or poems, there is a reference to meditation. If the word "his" is found ("his boat", "his cabin", etc.). . . there is a pointing to Thoreau.

It was Thoreau's belief that scientific instruments, of themselves, gave a distorted view of Nature. He long maintained a concept of Man-producing-art by recording intuitions through the use of Nature symbols, so . . . if the material on each page is contemplated directly and with enough sincerity, the poem will reveal of itself. There is no attempt to say "everything" and nothing to conceal. It is only the pond that can speak.

Close enough or far enough, let us see that "awareness" is present in Nature Herself, an awareness that requires no purpose . . . and reading-at-the-edge, perhaps we can allow ourselves "to be" without having to be somebody.

The "pictures" when settled are themselves moment-to-moment awakenings of mind . . . a passing of the water in the night.

How to bring the words that speak of Nature? A Nature that is always belonging . . . a Nature that is always incomplete.

Read and return! This is living as it is. This is living when we truly are alive.

All those ponds that never moved, and today I bring them home to move forever!

Vincent Tripi

"It is an experience of infinite beauty on which we unfailingly draw, which enables us to exaggerate ever truly."

THOREAU
Journal

P R O L O G U E

North Midnight to Brad's

From Goffstown, there is a road craving boulder to a ridge. Farther south, no roads exist at all. Dark-mud going, length-of-breath thickened by bracken and cone. Drifting like dust—we understand the mountain in our eyes.

Sharp northern breezes sharp. A Scarlet Cup beside the wheel. One by one, rocks tumble . . . the endless mist of shadow to a granite wall. Above us, tips of woodsmoke had wandered into masks, while the cabin slumbered . . . to wrestle with a falcon's cry.

A green-bushy-sunset, belonging to a belt of pine. Warblers and veery, wet through the hemlock, set out to hide the song. From the west, a spark of bridled silver was all that could be seen of Uncanunnuc. It did not change, the light that made us one.

My friend looked-off. In the path of his gaze, for the strongest winds . . . the sound of earth resolved the eastern sky. No ship had ever sailed our course—away.

Nine p.m. sitting: incense past stone water bowl, and wild again.

Dawn . . . the sun rising to the smell of oak. Crows begin to sink a trail of white across the col. By a corner of the garden, the tracks of a bear. My friend would be leaving all alone.

Tree buds—
Yellow-red
Leaves in my shoe!

Goffstown, N. H.
May 6, 1984

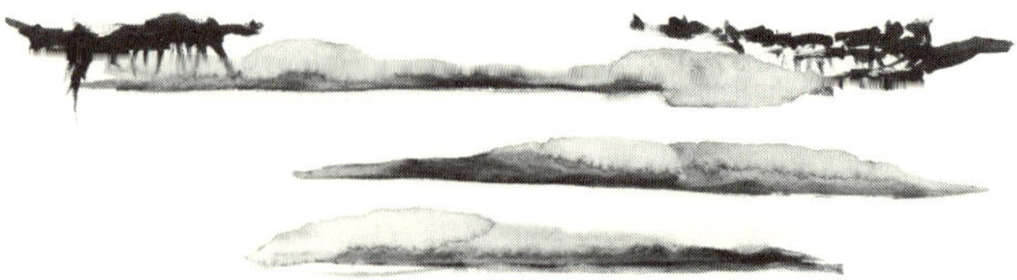

Lips to a Pond

"I should be pleased to meet a man in the woods. I wish he were to be encountered like wild caribous and moose."

THOREAU
Journal

Solitude was the face in whose smile . . . my eyes began to find themselves again.

Journal
May 7, 1984

"That sweet solitude my spirit seemed so early to require at once gave the preference to this recess among the pines, where almost sunshine and shadow were the only inhabitants that varied the scene, over that tumultuous and varied city, as if it had found its proper nursery."

THOREAU
Journal

At seven—
His past
Was the pond!

Years

The pond surrounding.
Many years lost
holding
earth beneath the sky.
Leaves fall . . . the color of a bird.
Cloud-self
as water goes by.

Old men should be ponds!
I'll be Sandy?*
Andromeda?*

Walden?

Journal
September 30, 1984

*Two small ponds near Walden.

Early Spring!
Tiny red bud—
"Where I lived . . ."*

"I am not alone, if I stand by myself. Who knows where in space this globe is rolling? Yet we will not give ourselves up for lost, let it go where it will."

THOREAU
A Week

No trace,
Of a black-fly
Out the door.

Tuliptree—
Green or gold?
Alone.

*Title of the second chapter in Walden.

The haze—
A rose returns,
A butterfly asleep.

"It was solitude with light; which is better than darkness."

THOREAU
A Walk to Wachusett

"Jewel
On my forehead
Firefly."

"On these mountain-summits, or near them, you find small and almost uninhabited ponds, sources of rivers, still and cold, strange and condensed clouds . . . of which nevertheless you make tea!"

THOREAU
Journal

By tea brewed—
Lips
To a pond.

"How fortunate were we who did not own an acre of these shores, who had not renounced our title to the whole. What I see is mine."

THOREAU
A Week

Parent
And child
On the bottom.

for Nathan, Lyn and John

Beavers—
He is all willow,
She is all pine.

for Dot Kronyak

Water Watched

Out! . . . from so near, from the hand of the westward evening star. Water watched, a fly's giant air—the last sound hangs cymbal over blue.

Along the mossy tresses, coming-wetness for the beauty of a shining stared-away . . . to hold my moonlight's blossom, leaf and stone.

Somewhere lies the wood for such a night.

In your eyes a hundred lilies yield a drop of sand. Behind me, too, a secret from the wind.

Drop of water
In my navel—
Leaving Walden Pond.

Journal
July 7, 1984

As close to the moon
As the firefly gets—
Beaver's nose.

One hand—
Eighteen sparrows
And a yellow bird.

for Peter Martel

Through a log
Pressing hazel—
Summer wind.

Journal
September 2, 1984

Not too much seeking for wisdom . . . and only to a Wood-duck's tail.

In silence where I stood there came a ripple—I sat and the ripple came again.

Wet vine
A boat
Hides the moon.

Journal
October 3, 1984

Autumn Falls

Autumn comes when she can. Calm days . . . the swift wings forgotten. Insects are crying, the silvery crying . . . a crack in the rock that is new. Do the tree frogs also hiding in the willow, hear cicada?

Power fans and toes around the falls. A salmon holds back a log—for a moment. Mist, low in the cedar, sends a shiver through my eyes. Oak leaves are they crimson—are they brown? Dragonflies, white at first, reveal the wind.

I work down between the paper birch and alder . . . leaning on a stick. The taste of the watercress grows. To the north, an Osprey diving—lengthens his life through a cloud.

A light-yellow sky. Walk in gold, the moon begins to pour . . . on one or two aspen stirring. With the evening breeze, the shadows of the beech trees reach an elm.

Great tombs lie empty, past embrace. Could tiny birds be sifting? Gently shawl, red into green.

Wooden duck—
Almost
Maple leaves.

Journal
September 20, 1984

"Ah, many a tale their color told! And gradually from week to week the character of each tree came out, and it admired itself reflected in the smooth mirror of the lake. Each morning the manager of this gallery substituted some new picture, distinguished by more brilliant or harmonious coloring, for the old upon the walls."

THOREAU
Walden

"It is a surprising and memorable, as well as valuable experience, to be lost in the woods any time . . . Not till we are lost, in other words not till we have lost the world, do we begin to find ourselves, and realize where we are and the infinite extent of our relations."

THOREAU
Walden

Path lost,
Bud-under
My feet!

One mosquito—
Had come this way
Before.

"The wildness of the savage is but a faint symbol of the awful ferity with which good men and lovers meet."

THOREAU
Walking

Trillium-white,
Lady's slipper-yellow—
Where we meet!
for Pat Sayers

The long day!
Kudzu leaf—
Bud.

"That one who does not stand so near to any man as to see the Divinity in him is truly alone."

THOREAU
Journal

Snow remains,
His boat, as if touching—
Birch and pine.

The hermit—
Two-axes
Christmas eve.

Alone,
A tree falls yesterday—
Today.

"There can be no very black melancholy to him who lives in the midst of nature and has his senses still."

THOREAU
Walden

A bird, just one,
A stone, just one—
Under the snow.

A single pine tree—
The old man hides his grey hairs
From the storm.

Envious—
Pond frozen
The end of the year.

"I would fain travel by a foot path round the world. This is the track of man alone."

THOREAU
Journal

The first track,
Buddha
In the snow.

for Al Hoffman

In our parting,
The snows on my boot
Melt-astray.

Clouds—
The bear and mouse
Have muddy feet.

Owl—

Back inside
the cabin

Mouse!

Snow on the mountain,
Poem, also in the fire—
Of Thoreau.

Shadow-moth
Wind
Out of flame.

The Question of Water

Teach me your age!
Flash of the snow
wearing down.
A bird sings,
but
then the well is dark.

Burrowing stillness.
Swing to what it gazes at . . .
slow-fast,
faces
when we breathe.

And the question of water . . .
Grip of a bucket,
Old as the sky.

Pumping water—
Sunset
At the sink.

Journal
April 5, 1985

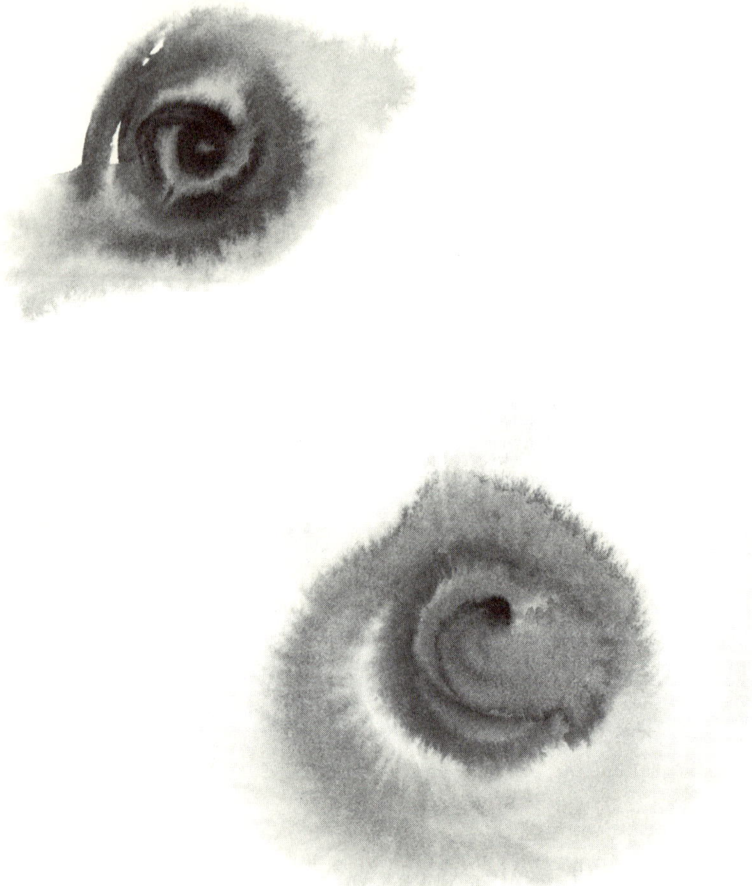

Two Moons

"Give me but the eyes to see the things which you possess."

THOREAU
Journal

Which eye is open wider? One said, "here it is" . . . instead of "I see this."

Journal
August 9, 1984

Walden Snow

Whispers-of-circle . . . Fairhaven,* Brister,* light's-child, who must winter climb.

The birch tower up. The trail is covered from the glen. Glint of mica, odd shiny yellow-black feather of sound. Through the willow, as if touching an antler, the weighted-down branch of an elm.

The pond seems to darken as a Wood duck swims away. A cedar log looks heavy, but it floats! In the laurel, deserted and still . . . the old boat a crystal by my hand.

Sunset from an oak . . . I fan the vision, the fire. How the earth smells when water drips down. A wren clutches smoke in its parting. Ponkawtasset*-wind!

These stone walls built snowed-on by storm.

Journal
December 1, 1984

The pond

blue
unknown
before

The wave.

for Walter Harding

"It is earth's eye looking into which the beholder measures the depth of his own nature."

THOREAU
Walden

Another pond?
Yet more snowflakes,
Not my face.

*Small hills near Concord, Massachusetts

"The sun was just setting behind the edge of a wooded hill, so rich a sunset as would never have ended but for some reason unknown to men, and to be marked with brighter colors than ordinary in the scroll of time."

THOREAU
A Week

Red-wing sunset—
The mallard
Adds a leaf.

for Kate Dougherty

Wild-geese-look
Shines
On the pond.

For Saying

Back to the night
for saying.
My feet as time
above the summer pond.
Gift from a dogwood,
great windows grasping . . .
still and grey—
the more deeply unmoveable wind.

The petal—
And no one knows who felt it,
Summer toes.

for Judy Cutler

Leaving traces on the water,
The wind
Where the white birch meet.

Journal
July 21, 1984

"After sunset the ponds are white and distinct."

THOREAU
Journal

White moon,
Snowman's shadow
Gone.

"How watchful we must be to keep the crystal well that we were made, clear."

THOREAU
Journal

The Way of Spruce

The way of spruce begins to glisten. Sleeper in things, the green-wet woodsmoke disappears.

It is enough to fill myself with clouds. A speckled alder, a broken willow . . . from the bottom.

Woodsmoke—
Dusk
In the grass-spider's web.

Journal
October 20, 1984

Breath

It is evening. Dust from an aspen blows over the grass. I think of the beaver. His face is the face of the pond.

Watched closely, the fireflies thin to where a Whip-poor-will has disappeared. A bullfrog cools, turned with mud from a heron's wing. Pine cones stop bobbing . . . a needle goes floating away.

I stept Autumn. Her long runs through the granite hills at twilight—a trail of any size. In the shadow of the mountain, a basswood tree becomes a tree of storm.

Silence drinks pure and all the nights lonely between it. Water, its new blade to the stone, the sky . . . not one left to throw at the moon.

Into red, into red—round the leaves how my breath begins to curl.

Ripples,
A maple holds more of—
The moon.

In the glance
Of a fish.

Journal
September 25, 1984

Scarecrow

This day on which the oak tree fell is drawing to a close. Noiselessly, a loon picks at random her feathers. Just-rock. Just-water. A beetle dims the sky.

Bent to the sound: east-fork, Old Brown's Creek,* Leach Hill,* into Bog-Hole* . . . overgrown! A dog-wood leaf that would not blow-away—the mallows!

Where I settle, the shadow of the pine: the only place that they had ever been. Ticks make a boulder. Autumn moon, everyday-in-stone.

I scarcely move at all.

Wind-within. It sits with me . . . the scarecrow on the hill.

Not his Journal,
But the winter wind
Is sad.

Journal
October 25, 1984

*Local geographic points.

Into the World

Face-by-face, stone-by-stone, I come to know the water. Fireflies—a spider's-web light green throughout the night.

Shadow over bud, so my love may flow into the world.

Midnight deer—
Orchid,
A shadow of horn.

Listening, Listening
Two moons
Underneath the falls.

Journal
June 2, 1984

"Nothing so fair, so pure, and at the same time so large, as a lake, perchance, lies on the surface of the earth. Sky water. It needs no fence. Nations come and go without defiling it. It is a mirror which no stone can crack . . . no dust can dim its surface ever fresh . . ."

THOREAU
Walden

A full moon,
Wet from the leaves
Round the pond.

Journal
October 1, 1984

The Walker

The fields own the wind where I walk! Moving slow. The last cloud stiff, where the poplars start to bend. Two deer cross, bringing whiteness back to life. Light-dark-light! By unfinished places, the distant snow returning what was mine.

Wild-geese had long since departed. Smoke from the chimney, old and shiny, just before the trail turns south. A chickadee's voice . . . as if it had noticed the mountain.

Echoed again near the hut! The swinging of a branch above? The walker neither speaks nor looks from right to left. The walker serves the walk.

Small-silver-step. Pine cones bouncing when the oak door closed . . . caught against a bit of sky, until the windows sparkled, and the desk and books were made of night.

Let no God appear—a candle for which to see the soul.

Candle—
Then
Lightning!

Journal
January 5, 1985

"What is nature unless there is an eventful human life passing within her? Many joys and many sorrows are the lights and shadows in which she shows most beautiful."

THOREAU
Journal

"Every man looks at his wood-pile with a kind of affection. I loved to have mine before my window, and the more chips the better to remind me of my pleasing work."

THOREAU
Walden

All night long—
Winter wood,
Layers of the moon.

Stars on the pond,
A shadow that comes
To my fireplace——goes!

"We must learn to reawaken and keep ourselves awake, not by mechanical aids, but by an infinite expectation of the dawn, which does not forsake us in our soundest sleep . . . To affect the quality of the day, that is the highest of arts."

THOREAU
Walden

Dawn
From the well,
Firefly!

"When I am most myself and see the clearest, men are least to be seen . . ."

THOREAU
Journal

The cold—
His cabin in the morning,
Basswood tree!

It's covered too!
Mirror for shaving—
Autumn pond.

"Standing in at the right angle, we are dazzled by the colors of the rainbow in colorless ice. From the right point of view, every storm and every drop in it is a rainbow."

THOREAU
Journal

With the sun—
Ice-bubbles
One on another.

The frogs,
And a great yawn—
Through the ice.

Journal
January 10, 1985

Light

One crow
Light
Across the field.
Nothing.
Missing nothing.
The earth supporting
Something
Deep inside me.

So quickly, a pick-axe
Clinging
To the Spring.

Journal
May 16, 1984

"We might try our lives by a thousand simple tests; as, for instance, that the same sun which ripens my beans illumines at once a system of earths like ours. If I had remembered this it would have prevented some mistakes. This is not the light in which I hoed them."

THOREAU
Walden

The bean-field—
Every bean
Was curved!

"Perhaps I can never find so good a setting for my thoughts as I shall thus have taken them out of. The crystal never sparkles more brightly than in the cavern."

THOREAU
Journal

Greatly shining—
Tree bud,
The nose of a bear.

How brilliant!
Mirror-taken
From the bottom.

My face in the water
Of a pitcher plant—
Distorted!

"Wisdom does not inspect, but behold. We must look a long time before we can see."

THOREAU
A Natural History of Massachusetts

Moment-of-fog——new tail!

A dozen or so, turtles—
One
Has turned to stone.

"Such is beauty ever, neither here nor there, now nor then, neither in Rome or in Athens, but wherever there is a soul to admire."

THOREAU
Journal

Spring
Snakeskin-seen
Cur
ls!

Solitude—
The glasses
Never fit.

Last in the Sky

"A man sits as many risks as he runs."
THOREAU
Walden

A new start
For each movement—
Above.

Journal
September 1, 1984

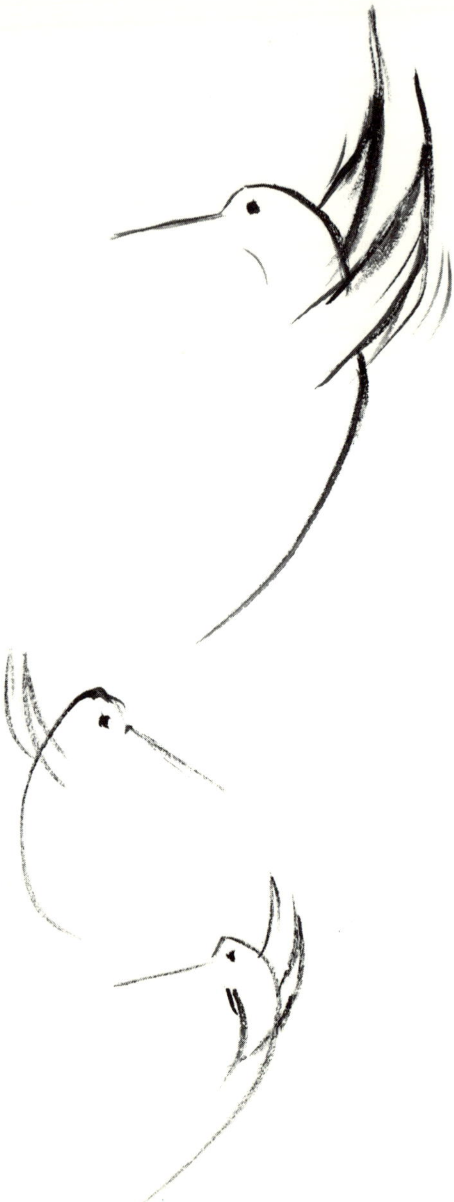

"Without outlet or inlet to the eye, it has still its history, in the lapse of its waves, in the rounded pebbles on its shore, and in the pines which grow down to its brink. It has not been idle, though sedentary, but like Abu Musa, teaches that 'Sitting still at home is the heavenly way; the going out is the way of the world.'"

THOREAU
A Winter Walk

Fire Wood
Pond!
Earth Metal

From the wind chimes,
A hummingbird—
Is dark

"All the world reposes in beauty to him who preserves equipoise in his life, and moves serenely on his path without secret violence . . ."

THOREAU
A Week

Meditation,
Mice also
On time.

Deep pickerel
Bubbles on—
Less.

I love
The first-last
Of the butterfly.

Stretching

Move
And the trees
Move too.
In a single pool,
blocking-out the sun . . .
Whirligig trying
to get out
to get in.
Black-faced skimmer
All that remains . . .
stretching
a petal
of dew.

With the dawn—
Beating tree tops,
The fires of spring.

Journal
May 11, 1984

"The art of life, of a poet's life, is, not having anything to do, to do something."

THOREAU
Journal

Snapping turtle
Stretches-out——bare trees!

Boulders

Ponds do not end!
There is no stillness till
noticed in a ripple . . .
No love till
water lapped the shore.

And the breath goes well.
Those great bottoms wait,
so I might be or
leave my boulders to
the wind.

The heron—
Unsettled
To be blue.

The fragrance—
A lily turns this way,
Turns that way.

Osprey
Flies fish-tail——behind!

Every now and then,
A young child will dawn—
From the berries.

"Of course!
He was holding-up his daughter
As the bluebirds flew away."
for Jack and Jenny

Deep-mud,
My shadow
Inside the canoe.

"Our most indifferent acts may be matter for secrecy, but whatever we do with utmost truthfulness and integrity, by virtue of its pureness, must be transparent as light."

THOREAU
A Week

Voices!—
Pressing one bud
With another.

Mirror hung,
A petal
Finds the wind.

"Actions are performed looking to virtue as a pilot looks to the motions of the stars . . ."

THOREAU
A Week

Searching for a dewdrop,
I found it by the paddle
Of a boat.

Carefully, Carefully,
Lowering a boat
Into the pond!

How soon !
Oars strike the water—
And an ant.

Wave

Reeds bringing rest.
Not-even leaves
In a small wooden boat.
A loon
            to the middle
            of the middle . . .
The wave
is a clear mark
Of dawn.

In the old wooden boat—
No traveller
Crossed.

May-cloud,
Walden
On the sail.

In memory of Henry Thoreau
May 6, 1984

Big

True, I was writing, and sometimes made haste to begin. Snatching-up the hand . . . water and sun, on a spot which from the first had been established for a friend.

They go on.

I sit as though the pond were very big.

Midday-sun,
Spider's legs
Cross.

Beetles—
One thorn
Blows away.

Journal
July 7, 1984

Older

Sometimes Nature brings a terrible, yet brilliant kind of beauty—the word *older*.

Where the sun drops . . . look, no one goes!

Not long ago a mirror. There were words for the darkness in our eyes.

A rock sinks,
The hot sun—
Nothing in the sky.

Journal
August 1, 1984

"So many autumn, ay, and winter days, spent outside the town, trying to hear what was in the wind, to hear and carry it express!"

THOREAU
Walden

Above the town—
One mallard lands, another
Warmer.

The Last Ice

The last ice caught in a blossom . . . melts slowly. Waters-of-spring, where the light is to be thrown away.

The yellow!—as a maple leaf comes from the bottom. Departing winter, have you seen your reflection in the pond?

The bullfrogs are silent . . . the lily pads begin to fade. Drops on the wing of a bird that has circled the moon. Along the surface, slivers of damp-stray air, as though the crystal of this spring performing, had kept for us all that had gone on below. A dog barks . . . the fish sink out of sight . . . the sky of New Hampshire is clear.

From a muddy bank, the fragrance of marigold, covered by tupelo, is swallowing a cloud. Young birds are restless, all along the redtop, every track of night has disappeared.

A spring breeze now led by the quail through an oak. Flyers at last! The first of all birds to fly.

A flight
From the pond—
Is longest.

Journal
June 9, 1985

Hands

Hands
In the winds
of home.
Rake for the rocks
of the mountain . . .
Pour forth the sweeping,
Play the death
which is lost in you
there.

Dusty-bird
Last
In the sky!

As the loon came down,
There was so much water
In the pond.

Standing still—
Passenger pigeon?*
The moon through a Chestnut tree?*

Journal
May 5, 1984

* Both species extinct now to the area.

"The great God is very calm withal. How superfluous is any excitement in his creatures."

THOREAU
Journal

Doe
Feeding fearful
Dries the dew.

Black-fly,
Round the curve
Of a turtle's shell.

Orchid,
To the moon!
Bumblebee.

Only the Swallows Have Worked

A muddy-burst of swallow!
You come out from the eyes
lost behind.
A bitter rock
        erosion
        the cloud-face
        the willows there
With all that moon
inside you,
        a memory
        a circle
        from the ground.
I look looking,
wet with wing
        and star,
        with song . . .
from breath of
earthparting.

                Swallows through blossoms,
            Mud
                In their beaks.

        Sunset—
    The spider's web
        Torn.

Journal
May 3, 1985

"What if all ponds were shallow? Would it not react on the minds of men? While men believe in the infinite some ponds will be thought to be bottomless."

THOREAU
Walden

Bell

I call it trail—empty now across the southern sky. And it awakens me, brought by the wind, a tree-bud enjoying the cool.

Dark against the dark, returns an echo . . . in such a way that one might utter rivers, say forest . . . that one might hear the secrets talk of now.

I sit sitting. Red hawk in the notch. Shadow lost, opening a cloud. A tree frog is one with its maple. Gulping-May, an orchid tossed with wing.

A firefly comes to my pine shelter . . . goes. From where it disappears, the mountains stir, then stirs, to be the sound of a distant bell. Loons thaw the water . . . all at once the shallow from the deep!

Still deeper,
Still deeper—
Walden Pond.

Journal
May 1, 1985

Thunder One Hand

"Silence is audible to all men, at all times, and in all places."

THOREAU
A Week

In the words, too, I am finding much. Silence that has made up its mind . . . to trust me.

Journal
December 29, 1984

"Silence is the universal refuge . . ."

THOREAU
A Week

This morning from a frog,
I hear all I need to hear—
About the pond!

"My profession is to be always on the alert to find God in nature, to know his lurking-places, to attend all the oratorios, the operas, in nature."

THOREAU
Journal

Cabin door
POP!
In July.

Days

When was it they were stars . . . these crystals? Ice is age! There, we become the flame; stand like maple, hold birdsong—Snow, in the days when space was young.

Morning—
Snowman
Faced the pond!

Journal
March 22, 1985

Wet

Wet-white-way. The sun turning back, in the eye of a Blue-winged teal.

Seeing everything with light . . . A pond that comes slowly. Slowly once again. "Zz-s-s-sszz", "Ss-z-z-zzss", and the snowflake of only one tail.

Wild mint seeds
Being-wetted
By a teal.

Journal
April 10, 1985

"The thrush alone declares the immortal wealth and vigor that is in the forest. Whenever a man hears it, he is young, and Nature is in her spring."

THOREAU
Journal

This-way, that-way,
The Wood thrush
A voice before Thoreau.

Still

I spot it at once . . . a striped-throated loon. The featherfoil is warm, the damselfly dripping.

Still—still—still!
My toe finds a crack inside the stone.

My Japanese flute—
Hurrying the black flies,
Summer breeze.

The silence—
Strings of cattail
Hang from yellow-beaks.

Journal
July 1, 1984

Young boy,
His name
In the nearest tree.
for Jesse Daniel Carr

Jet
At the pass—
Hollow elm!

Off the cabin
Struck by lightning,
Rubber ball.

"My heart leaps into my mouth at the sound of the wind in the woods. I whose life was but yesterday so desultory and shallow, suddenly recover my spirits, my spirituality, through my hearing."

THOREAU
Journal

Summer
Quickly!
From a child's first dive.

Cupping shells—
Her son's shirt stretched
Across the stone.

for Sushila and Luke

"Thus, for a long time, nature overlooks the encroachment and profanity of man. The wood still cheerfully and unsuspiciously echoes the strokes of the axe that fells it, and while they are few and seldom, they enhance its wildness, and all the elements strive to naturalize the sound."

THOREAU
A Winter Walk

Empty cabin,
Towhees scratch—
The autumn wind.

Path

Stream running young,
long ago.
The orchids know less
and less silence.
A Red-tail's cry . . . tree-word,
                              dust

above the pine.
There remains, perhaps some blossom
to be leaned-on
day after day.
My feet shall be as grass again,
standing on the path.
Because I'm for the path
Alone.

Orchid
Thunder
One hand!

Journal
June 9, 1984

Ice

Most tracks go unseen. The way set with hatpin and foil. Butterfly yet eager for the mountain . . . absolutely still. A tree bud, both new and not new.

I cannot hear to hear.

Breathing takes over—the water takes over. At the sound of the falls, the edge of the pine forest grows.

Bright-mists break the circle of the pond . . . silver and white above the stone. Glazed horsetail in a long woven-cloth of empty light. Under last night's moon, a thousand stars had trickled through the ice!

"Crack!"
With me
Walks on the pond.

Journal
April 30, 1985

"In this lonely glen with its creased ice and crystals of all hues, our lives are more serene and worthy to contemplate."

THOREAU
A Winter Walk

"When, as was commonly the case, I had none to commune with, I used to raise the echoes by striking with a paddle on the side of my boat, filling the surrounding woods with circling and dilating sound, stirring them up as the keeper of a menagerie his wild beast, until I elicited a growl from every wooded vale and hill-side."

THOREAU
Walden

Echo—
Climbs the mountain
Swims the pond.

"Row, brothers, row,
"Row, brothers, row"*—
Again!

for Michael Campbell-Drexler

*Canadian Boat Song, one of Thoreau's favorites

Chants

This is what Nature wants to restore in us: that breathless harmony in which her voice becomes ours and our voice hers, and it seems blessed just to walk in her shadow . . . her light shining-out from our eyes.

Chants of the forest—I listen, to answer my soul.

Thunder——The decoy
Left staring!

A pine cone
Not landing on the lily—
But the stone.

Journal
June 5, 1984

"All sound heard at the greatest possible distance produces one and the same effect, a vibration of the Universal lyre . . ."

THOREAU
Walden

Geese honk—
High
Above the map.

Children

There is a path, long enough for its beginning . . . for the silence of our lives.

Surely in the waves, a great ship to take us away . . . the kind that children build.

Children's boat
Bounces
The moon.

for
Gabriel
Tim
Kanoa
Ryland
Jeffrey
Brett and . . .
Nessy!

Journal
August 15, 1984

Evening hive—
Apple blossoms
Fall.

"You must walk so gently as to hear the finest sounds, the faculties being in repose. Your mind must not perspire."

THOREAU
Journal

Under hooves,
The sound
In moonlight, of stone.

A mallard's beak turned sideways—
I will listen to
The rain.

"Silence alone is worthy to be heard. A night in which the silence was audible. I hear the unspeakable."

THOREAU
Journal

Silence—
The cardinals
Never part.

Toward Everything

I walk the meadow—toward everything! Sounds of disappearing dry the dew. A dogwood I can't see. A ladybug, not-ready, flying.

Coming to a ledge, the loons diving down . . . being seen diving down. For the flicker, a perfect place to settle, soft-wind through the hidden pine.

Pickerel in the cool, heedless of a bullfrog's croaking. A single leaf on the branch where a chickadee sings.

Looking out across the water, now in the light . . . now in the darkness, a swallow.

The heron leads its shadow from the pond.

Stars behind buckle lean back against the mountain wall. Spring, as though someone gave a life for it and more . . . our flowers grow bigger and big!

Iris, marigold
trillium, clover
yellow-lady's slipper—

Prayer!

Journal
May 10, 1984

". . . flowers as well as weeds follow in the footsteps of man."

THOREAU
A Winter Walk

Her Eyes

Now—leaves, boulders, breath-and-cloud are child!

On a trail lost for years, where chestnut once grew to an acre, when ginseng fell, as the mountain passed around a cup-of-sky.

Because of the pond—the silence of the pond.

Pine cones—webbed to a soft circle . . . blur.

Shining from a tortoise in the night. Nearby, an owl sits waiting—where the moonlight should be.

A mighty snow reflected in her eyes.

White snow—
White
Owl's pass.

Journal
November 5, 1985

What the Hawk Sees

Sense of his
handle's Way
silent
brings a wind.
What the hawk sees . . . cloud of breath or
drop of ancient water,
Leaving nothing——behind.

Ice-chopping
Nearest
The sky!

Journal
January 1, 1985

The Fire

Here is the start of Winter—stone of Her empty field; eagle's-cloud, eyes for all we know, awake as wind. When was the moment when no more snow came? His life from which a track appeared?

Climbing toward midnight, the old man crossed the creek bed, turning uphill on a fading ridge . . . long drifts, a plough against the wall.

And the red deer followed. Their breathing like amice, or lantern—the trail of a saffron robe.

The grey rocks through the pokeweed are sharpened by shadow. Somewhere in the distance, his silence now part of the storm.

Fire, come when you should! Bent-oak on footsteps listen—with long spun echoes melting song.

What are we near to? Winter is all that he has been.

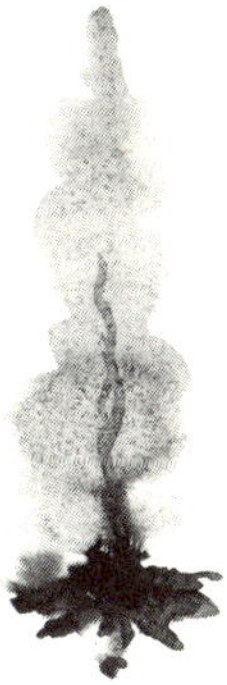

The fire—
Two branches
Bent by an eagle.

Journal
December 24, 1984

"There is a slumbering subterranean fire in Nature which never goes out, and which no cold can chill. This subterranean fire has its altar in each man's breast . . . A healthy man, indeed, is the complement of the seasons, and in winter, summer is in his heart."

THOREAU
A Winter Walk

Walden

"True, our converse a stranger
is to speech;
Only the practiced ear can catch
the surging words
That break and die upon thy
pebbled lips."

THOREAU
Poem 1838

The pond
Says nothing—
In the shell.

". . . after each sound which near at hand broke the stillness of the night, each crackling of the twigs, or rustling among the leaves, there was a sudden pause, and a deeper and more conscious silence . . ."

THOREAU
A Week

The breeze,
Raindrops——from willow,
from pine.

Mosquitoes—
The cabin door
Squeak!

"Completely silent and attentive I will be this hour, and the next, and forever."

THOREAU
Journal

Bluebells—
I have the perfect book
With which to press them.

"This is the most the bookmaker can attain to. If he make his volume a mole whereon the waves of silence may break, it is well."

THOREAU
A Week

Poems

The last of the cattail!

I push them aside with my nose. Wind through the cedar, catches moonlight-off-the-ice. Rumbles-by!—the foxtail is a storm. Tomorrow, I may speak. It is snowflakes that give the best poems.

Journal
December 25, 1984

Sail

Watching-water is the pond,
a long deeper breath
under sail.
Ship behind living, or if
mountain will grow . . . All
of one perfect away.
In the palm of my hand
The sound
has it been hiding,
all this time?
Earth is our Mother!
Count-ripples.
Go-light . . .
The edge of the pond
was man!

Where you always face—
A pond
May soon appear!

GASSHŌ

To my many friends who report no knowledge of Yoga or Zen, but share a spirit in their eyes.

To my New Hampshire neighbors, who gave water, books, candles, rice . . . whatever I needed to continue on my Way.

To George and Nancy Carr for their gift of wisdom.

To my parents whose light was never dim.

To my sister whose poetry is lived.

To Malcolm Margolin for the first word that he said.

To Sarah Levin . . . for shining.

To Brad both old and both new!

To Shunryu Suzuki Roshi.

To Bashō . . . the thunder of his hand.

To my great friend Cathy Hill without whom I would have taken down my sail before the storm.

To Beginners one and all!

July 12, 1987
San Francisco

PHOTO: LINDA KAY

About the Author

Vincent Shankar Tripi keeps books by their color, has been known to hoard morels . . . and goes barefoot as much as he can.

Since 1980 he has taught Yoga and meditation, and for 15 years worked with children in group-homes and residential treatment centers.

He is at present completing a book about The White Mountains of New Hampshire.

About the Artist

Linda Clarke Kneeland is a painter and journalist who resides in rural Pennsylvania with her husband and two daughters.

Others living inside her are the teacher, mother, singer, musician, woman . . . and lover of Nature.